96 Facts ABOUT BAD BUNNY

Quizzes, QUOTES, QUESTIONS, and MORE!

BY ARIE KAPLAN

ILLUSTRATED BY Risa Rodil

Grosset & Dunlap

GROSSET & DUNLAP
An imprint of Penguin Random House LLC, New York

First published in the United States of America by Grosset & Dunlap,
an imprint of Penguin Random House LLC, New York, 2024

Text copyright © 2024 by Arie Kaplan
Illustrations copyright © 2024 by Risa Rodil

Photo credits: used throughout: (speech bubbles with question marks)
Oleksandr Melnyk/iStock/Getty Images

GROSSET & DUNLAP is a registered trademark of
Penguin Random House LLC.

Visit us online at penguinrandomhouse.com.

Manufactured in Canada

ISBN 9780593754665   10 9 8 7 6 5 4 3 2 1 FRI

Design by Kimberley Sampson

TABLE OF CONTENTS

Part 1

FROM BENITO TO BUNNY

Icon and Phenomenon

Ever since he released his self-produced hit single "Diles" in 2016, Bad Bunny has taken the music world by storm. First he became a superstar in Latin America. Shortly afterward, he became a phenomenon who was famous the world over. By achieving fame, he helped bring musical genres like Latin trap and reggaeton to a wider audience.

Bad Bunny has also smashed established gender norms with his sense of style. To him, fashion is genderless, fluid, and free, and people should dress in whatever way they like. In fact, Bad Bunny has become equally known for the creativity of his lyrics and the inclusivity of his message.

But who is Bad Bunny, really? How did he start out in the music industry? Just how prolific *is* he, as an artist?

If you'd like to know the answers to those questions, and many more, read on!

FAST FACTS!

Reggaeton is a fusion of Latin music, North American hip-hop, and reggae.

Latin trap music is a type of Spanish-language music that is influenced by Black culture in general, and Southern hip-hop in particular.

Ever Since He Was Five Years Old

As you might have suspected, Bad Bunny's real name isn't actually "Bad Bunny." It's Benito Antonio Martínez Ocasio. Benito was born in the pueblo of Almirante Sur in Vega Baja, Puerto Rico, on March 10, 1994. His father, Tito Martínez, was a truck driver, and his mother, Lysaurie Ocasio, was a schoolteacher.

Ever since he was five years old, Benito wanted to be a singer. So when he was young, his mother took him to church, where he sang in the children's choir. And by the time he was in high school, Benito had started freestyle rapping to entertain his friends.

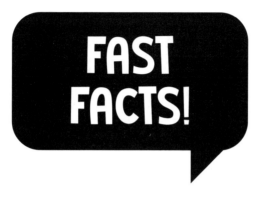

FAST FACTS!

Benito is the oldest of three siblings. His brothers are Bernie and Bysael.

"Pueblo" is a Spanish word that means "city."

Signed!

When Benito was around six years old, his teacher told him to dress up in a bunny costume for Easter. According to Benito, he dressed up in the costume but wasn't happy about it. That was how he earned the nickname "Bad Bunny."

Many years later, when Benito was attending the University of Puerto Rico at Arecibo, he spent his free time posting his own songs on SoundCloud. He needed a stage name, and he went with "Bad Bunny."

In 2016, Bad Bunny posted the synth-trap single "Diles" on SoundCloud. "Diles" caught the attention of DJ Luian, an entertainment entrepreneur who owned a record label called Hear This Music. DJ Luian signed Bad Bunny to his label.

It was finally happening! Bad Bunny was a professional singer, just like he'd always dreamed!

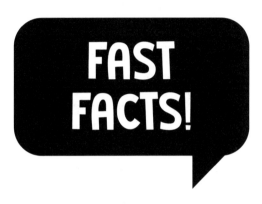

FAST FACTS!

Bad Bunny has *also* said that he chose the "Bad Bunny" stage name because no matter how bad he behaves, he has a cute face.

When Bad Bunny was going to college at the University of Puerto Rico at Arecibo, he was studying communications.

"Soy Peor"

In 2016, shortly after Bad Bunny released "Diles," he dropped the angst-ridden trap ballad "Soy Peor." This is often considered his first hit song because it reached No. 19 on *Billboard*'s Hot Latin Songs chart.

"Soy Peor" is a breakup anthem. It's about someone who has broken up with their significant other and is bitter, upset, and anxious to move on with their life. But even though "Soy Peor" is a sad song, its success made Bad Bunny very happy!

FAST FACTS!

"Soy Peor" means "I'm Worse" in Spanish.

By June of 2017, the music video for "Soy Peor" racked up 205 million views on YouTube.

Did You Know That . . .

1 When Bad Bunny was attending college, he made money in his spare time by bagging groceries at an ECONO supermarket.

2 The song title "Diles" means "Tell Them" in Spanish.

3 In 2017, Bad Bunny released a remixed version of "Soy Peor," featuring fellow recording artists J Balvin, Ozuna, and Arcángel.

4 By March of 2023, the music video for "Soy Peor" hit one billion views on YouTube.

5 At the time, it was the tenth Bad Bunny music video to hold that distinction.

6 Reggaeton is a genre of music that was created in Puerto Rico, in the underground club scene, during the 1990s.

7 The Latin trap subgenre began with Latin trappers dropping their rhymes on top of well-known hip-hop beats.

8 Trap music in general is not as easily defined as Latin trap. It can be music that's influenced by street-oriented hip-hop.

9 But it can also be defined as dance floor–oriented music.

10 Trap music often has a signature sound, which can involve jittery hi-hats, loud tom fills, and booming drums.

Feet on the Ground

"I always thank God that me, my friends and my family maintain our feet on the ground."

—Bad Bunny on being grounded

Who are the people in your life who make you feel grounded and relaxed? Are they your family members? Your friends? Your fellow students at school? Write about them on the lines below.

_____

_____

_____

_____

_____

_____

_____

_____

_____

_____

_____

_____

_____

_____

_____

_____

_____

_____

_____

Costume Chaos

When Bad Bunny was a child, his teacher told him to wear a bunny costume for Easter. He wore the costume but regretted it. What is the cheesiest, corniest, or silliest costume you've ever worn? It can be something you wore for Halloween, for a costume party, or for some other reason entirely. Write about it on the lines below.

_____

_____

_____

_____

_____

_____

_____

_____

_____

_____

_____

_____

_____

_____

_____

_____

_____

_____

Quick Quiz: Finding His Way

1) Which reggaeton singer did Bad Bunny like to listen to on the radio when he was growing up?

   a. Richie Rich
   b. Casper the Friendly Ghost
   c. Little Dot
   d. Tego Calderón

2) When Bad Bunny was a child, he and his family used to take a car trip to a lavish shopping mall in San Juan a few times a year. What was that mall called?

   a. Plaza las Américas
   b. Star City
   c. Gotham City
   d. Central City

3) When Bad Bunny was growing up, he used to hang out at a small ____ ____ in Vega Baja.

   a. Candy jungle
   b. Mitten farm
   c. Skate park
   d. Zipper ocean

4) When Bad Bunny was a kid, he was fascinated with professional ____.

a. Ham
b. Wrestling
c. Pork
d. Bacon

5) Bad Bunny usually sings and raps in a distinctive ____ voice.

a. Silent
b. Noiseless
c. Inaudible
d. Baritone

Check your answers on page 78!

Part II

COMPOSING AND COLLABORATING

A Celebration of Femininity

Bad Bunny became more well-known as a result of "Soy Peor." Because of that, other Latinx artists invited him to collaborate with them. In 2017, he was the featured artist on Colombian singer Karol G's song "Ahora Me Llama" (in English, "Now He's Calling Me"). The song was a celebration of the power of femininity, and it reached number ten on the *Billboard* Hot Latin Songs chart.

FAST FACTS!

"Ahora Me Llama" was mentioned as one of the "Songs of 2017" on the year-end round-up for NPR's "Alt.Latino" blog.

In October 2017, Karol G released a remix of "Ahora Me Llama," featuring a new verse by Quavo (best known as part of the Atlanta rap group Migos).

Trap Kingz

In late 2017, Bad Bunny hosted the first six episodes of the radio show *Trap Kingz*, produced by Apple Music's global radio station Beats 1. *Trap Kingz* was Beats 1's first Spanish-language show. In the show, Bad Bunny discussed the trap movement, and he also introduced music from his Latin trap colleagues like Arcángel, Farruko, and Noriel.

Bad Bunny's hosting duties on *Trap Kingz* established him as someone to watch in the music industry and increased his exposure. Clearly, his star was on the rise.

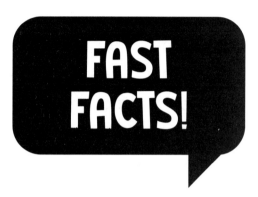

FAST FACTS!

When announcing Bad Bunny's hosting duties on *Trap Kingz* in November of 2017, *Billboard Magazine* called him "one of the most in-demand trap singers."

In 2018, Bad Bunny's remix of his song "Te Boté" (featuring Ozuna and Nicky Jam) hit number one on the *Billboard* Hot Latin Songs chart. In English, "Te Boté" means "I Threw You Out."

An Invitation from Cardi B

At this point in Bad Bunny's career, he'd mostly worked with other artists from Latin American countries. That changed in 2018, when he was invited to be a featured artist on American rapper Cardi B's song "I Like It," alongside fellow featured artist J Balvin. The song appeared on Cardi's debut album *Invasion of Privacy*. "I Like It" was incredibly popular, and eleven weeks after hitting the charts, it climbed up to number one on the *Billboard* Hot 100.

Bad Bunny's collaboration with Cardi B took his fame to another level. "I Like It" made him a truly international artist and gave him much more exposure in the United States.

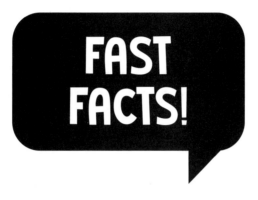

FAST FACTS!

"I Like It" included a sample of Pete Rodriguez's classic hit song "I Like It Like That."

In July 2018, the website Remezcla announced that "I Like It" was the number one song in the country.

A Unique Christmas Gift

By the end of 2018, Bad Bunny had released several hit singles. Some of them were solo efforts. On others, he was collaborating with fellow artists. But he had yet to drop an album. When would it happen?

Then in an exclusive interview with *Billboard* on December 23, 2018, Bad Bunny announced that the following day—Christmas Eve—he would be surprise-releasing his debut album.

The album in question was called *X 100PRE*. The title was an acronym for "Por Siempre," which means "Forever" in Spanish. It was appropriate that Bad Bunny released *X 100PRE* just in time for Christmas, because the album was essentially a gift to his fans: It contained fifteen tracks, many of which were brand-new.

X 100PRE was a massive success both critically and commercially. It won rave reviews, and it was Bad Bunny's first project to hit number one on the *Billboard* Top Latin Albums chart.

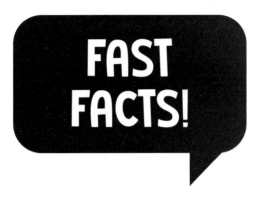

FAST FACTS!

X 100PRE also featured three collaborations: "200 MPH" (featuring Diplo), "La Romana" (featuring El Alfa), and "Mía" (featuring Drake).

"Mía" was initially released as a single in October 2018, two months before *X 100PRE* dropped.

Did You Know That . . .

1 Bad Bunny has known his deejay, DJ Orma, since they were both in tenth grade.

2 Karol G's real name is Carolina Giraldo Navarro.

3 "I Like It" wasn't Bad Bunny's first collaboration with Colombian singer J Balvin.

4 In 2017, Bad Bunny and J Balvin had collaborated with Prince Royce on the song "Sensualidad."

5 Prince Royce is Dominican, but he was born in the United States.

6 "Sensualidad" means "Sensuality" in Spanish.

7 Pete Rodriguez's song "I Like It Like That" was first released in 1967.

8 Bad Bunny rapped in both English and Spanish on "I Like It."

9 In 2019, the *Nation* proclaimed, "Like him or not, Bad Bunny is *the* pop star for our times."

10 Bad Bunny's song "Mía" was the first full Spanish-language song to hit the number one spot on the Top Songs chart for Apple Music in the United States.

Hopes and Dreams

"[M]y dad is proud of me and is happy that I feel good and that I'm living my dreams."

—Bad Bunny on his hopes and dreams

What are your dreams? What would you like to do for a living when you grow up? Would you like to be a rapper or a singer like Bad Bunny? Would you like to do something else? Write about your hopes and dreams on the lines below.

_____

_____

_____

_____

_____

_____

_____

_____

_____

_____

_____

_____

_____

_____

_____

_____

_____

_____

_____

Your Very Own Radio Show!

    In the early days of his career, Bad Bunny hosted the first few episodes of the radio show *Trap Kingz*. Do you think it would be fun to host your own radio show? What subject would your show be about? Write about it on the lines below.

_____

_____

_____

_____

_____

_____

_____

_____

_____

_____

_____

_____

_____

_____

_____

_____

_____

_____

_____

Quick Quiz: Growing Fame and Acclaim

1) How many views did the music video for "Mía" get during its first twenty-four hours on YouTube?

   a. Two views
   b. Four views
   c. Twelve million views
   d. Negative six views

2) Bad Bunny's music is sometimes described as ____ ____, which is a general, all-encompassing term for the contemporary Latinx urban-music movement

   a. Música urbana
   b. Cool stuff
   c. Good stuff
   d. Nice stuff

3) One of the songs on *X 100PRE* is "Tenemos Que Hablar" (in English, "We Have to Talk"), which could be described as a ____ song.

   a. Singy
   b. Songish
   c. Songesque
   d. Humorous

4) Bad Bunny's song "La Romana" is about the city of La Romana, which is in the ____ ____.

a. Southwest side
b. Dominican Republic
c. Northwest side
d. Northeast side

5) Bad Bunny's song "200 MPH" was produced by . . .

a. Mr. Mxyzptlk
b. Mr. Mind
c. Diplo
d. Mr. Monster

Check your answers on page 78!

THREE ALBUMS, THREE MASTERWORKS

A Very Busy Year

During the global COVID-19 pandemic, some people understandably took time off to look inward and reexamine their lives. Others spent the extended time indoors making art. Bad Bunny was one of those people. In 2020, he released three albums. As Bad Bunny told *Daily Show* host Trevor Noah, he loves music and couldn't stop making it, even during the pandemic.

But this sustained burst of creativity didn't simply give Bad Bunny a way to cope during a global crisis. Those three albums were of such high quality that by the time people began emerging from their homes in the latter days of the pandemic, Bad Bunny wasn't just a star. He was a megastar.

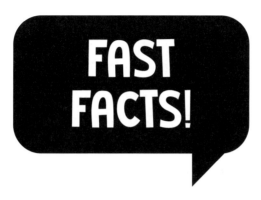

FAST FACTS!

On the *Billboard* Year-End charts in December 2020, Bad Bunny was named Top Latin Artist and Top Latin Male Artist of 2020.

This was the second consecutive year in which Bad Bunny held those titles.

The Initials Stand for . . .

On February 29, 2020, Bad Bunny released his second solo studio album, *YHLQMDLG*. The album title's initials stand for "Yo Hago Lo Que Me Da La Gana" (in English, "I Do Whatever I Want"). One of the most acclaimed songs to come out of *YHLQMDLG* was "Yo Perreo Sola."

Earlier in his career, through songs like "Ahora Me Llama," Bad Bunny celebrated the power of femininity. But he furthered his commitment to feminism with "Yo Perreo Sola" (which means "I Dance Alone"). The song was a powerful statement against misogynistic violence and sexual harassment.

In the music video for "Yo Perreo Sola," Bad Bunny appeared in a red vinyl dress and matching boots. In doing so, he was questioning outdated ideas of what it is to be stereotypically masculine.

But the "Yo Perreo Sola" music video was far from the only time Bad Bunny dressed in drag or expressed his gender-fluid fashion sense. Over the years, he's worn pink minidresses and colorful nail polish. He refuses to bow to traditional gender norms.

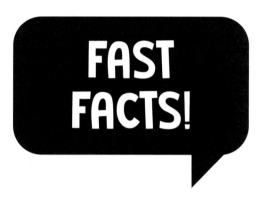

FAST FACTS!

In 2021, Bad Bunny won his first Grammy Award for *YHLQMDLG*.

Specifically, *YHLQMDLG* won a Grammy for Best Latin Pop or Urban Album.

Surprise!

Bad Bunny's second project of 2020 was *Las Que No Iban A Salir*, a compilation album he surprise-released in May of that year. The title of the album, *Las Que No Iban A Salir*, means "The Ones That Were Not Coming Out." As with *X 100PRE*, he gave the general public very little warning before the album's release.

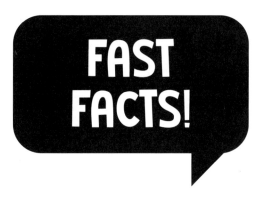

FAST FACTS!

Las Que No Iban A Salir features appearances by many of Bad Bunny's fellow reggaeton artists, such as Don Omar, Nicky Jam, Zion & Lennox, Yandel, and Jhayco.

Before *Las Que No Iban A Salir* came out, Bad Bunny previewed songs from it during a three-hour appearance on his Instagram Live.

The Last Tour of the World

Bad Bunny's third and final album of 2020 was *El Último Tour Del Mundo*. In English, the album's title translates to "The Last Tour of the World." When writing and recording songs for this album, Bad Bunny envisioned himself a decade in the future—at his final world tour in 2030—and he tried to imagine the music he'd play on that tour.

But the creation of *El Último Tour Del Mundo* wasn't just inspired by Bad Bunny musing about what the songs on his final world tour might sound like. According to *Rolling Stone* magazine, the dark, brooding vibe of some of the songs on the album—like the trap anthem "Hoy Cobré" (in English, "Today I Got Paid")—was inspired by the grief and isolation of the pandemic.

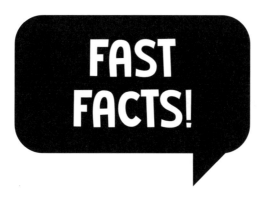

FAST FACTS!

Bad Bunny made history with *El Último Tour Del Mundo*, which was the first-ever number one Spanish-language album on *Billboard*'s album chart.

El Último Tour Del Mundo largely consists of reggaeton and trap music, but the songs on the album were also influenced by a host of other musical genres, like electronic, rock, and new wave music.

Did You Know That . . .

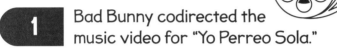

1 Bad Bunny codirected the music video for "Yo Perreo Sola."

2 The message of both the song "Yo Perreo Sola" and its accompanying music video is that if women want to dance alone, safely, and unbothered by men, they should be able to do just that.

3 February 29, the day *YHLQMDLG* was released on, is also known as leap day.

4 It's called that because February only has twenty-nine days once every four years.

5 A calendar year containing an extra day in February is called a leap year.

6 During non-leap years, February has twenty-eight days.

7 *YHLQMDLG* debuted at No. 2 on the *Billboard* 200.

8 That made it the highest-charting all-Spanish-language album ever (at the time).

9 On *El Último Tour Del Mundo*, the song "La Noche de Anoche" (in English, "The Night of Last Night") featured the Spanish singer Rosalía.

10 Legendary rapper Snoop Dogg appeared in the music video for Bad Bunny's song "Hoy Cobré."

This Is Who I Am

"This is who I am. This is my music. This is my culture. If you don't like it, don't listen to me. If you like it, you know."

—Bad Bunny on himself

What is your favorite thing about the culture or traditions that have been passed down to you by your family? It could be a song, a custom, a work of literature, a holiday, or a favorite food. Write about it on the lines below.

_____

_____

_____

_____

_____

_____

_____

_____

_____

_____

_____

_____

_____

_____

_____

_____

_____

_____

_____

_____

Prolific

Bad Bunny is a very prolific singer, rapper, and songwriter. To be "prolific" means that you produce a great amount or number of something. For Bad Bunny, he is prolific in the number of albums and songs he creates. Is there an area of your life in which you're prolific? Are you a prolific writer? A prolific reader? A prolific musician? A prolific athlete? Write about it on the lines below.

_____

_____

_____

_____

_____

_____

_____

_____

_____

_____

_____

_____

_____

_____

_____

Quick Quiz: A Great Amount or Number

1) **What is the title of *YHLQMDLG*'s final track?**

   a. "<3"
   b. "Sergeant Pepper's Lonely Hearts Club Band"
   c. "Eleanor Rigby"
   d. "Love Me Do"

2) **In the music video for "Hoy Cobré," Bad Bunny is seen trying to keep his balance on top of a moving ____.**

   a. Octopus
   b. Antelope
   c. Skunk
   d. Truck

3) **The ten tracks on *Las Que No Iban a Salir* include ____ from previous recording sessions.**

   a. Snakes
   b. Outtakes
   c. Rakes
   d. Lakes

4) Bad Bunny's song "Dákiti" is named after San Juan's Dákiti ____.

a. Robots
b. Leprechauns
c. Beach
d. Mermaids

5) Bad Bunny has collaborated with three of the following musical legends. Which one has he NOT collaborated with?

a. Nicki Minaj
b. Ricky Martin
c. Sy Snootles
d. Marc Anthony

Check your answers on page 78!

Part IV

THE PERFORMANCE(S) OF A LIFETIME
Across All Media

Over the past three years, Bad Bunny has stretched his wings as a performer. Not only has he made more music, but he's also tried his hand at pro wrestling and acting in films and television shows! And his live shows are spectacular events one truly has to see in person.

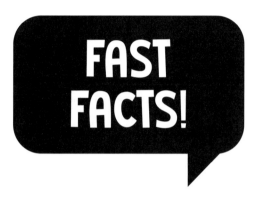

FAST FACTS!

From 2020 to 2022, Bad Bunny was the most-streamed recording artist in the world on Spotify.

In 2022, Irish publication *JOE* called Bad Bunny "arguably the most famous person in the world right now."

From Rapper to ... Wrestler?

From very early in his career, Bad Bunny has been a wrestling fan. In 2017, he even got wrestling icon Ric Flair to appear in the music video for his song "Chambea" (in English, "Reload"). And in 2020, one of the songs on Bad Bunny's album *El Último Tour Del Mundo* was titled "Booker T," after the legendary wrestler of the same name. The following year, Bad Bunny participated in a tag team match at the 2021 WrestleMania event. That's right, Bad Bunny entered the ring as a pro wrestler!

But the story of Bad Bunny's wrestling career doesn't end there. In May of 2023, Bad Bunny won his first solo match at the WWE Backlash event in San Juan, Puerto Rico.

Will Bad Bunny's wrestling career continue to blossom? Only time will tell!

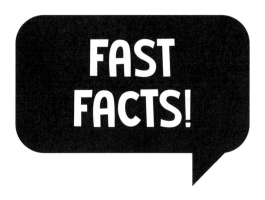

FAST FACTS!

At the 2023 WWE Backlash event, Bad Bunny's opponent was Damian Priest.

Damian Priest was Bad Bunny's tag team partner at WrestleMania 2021.

Making Movies

When he was a young child in Puerto Rico, Bad Bunny hoped to one day make music *and* movies. In the 2020s, he started to pursue acting roles. After a small cameo in the 2021 film *F9: The Fast Saga* and a recurring role as gangster Arturo "Kitty" Páez in the final season of the Netflix series *Narcos: Mexico* (also in 2021), he had his first major supporting role in a film in the 2022 Brad Pitt movie *Bullet Train*.

An action-packed, comedic heist film about a bunch of criminals who fight one another while traveling in the titular vehicle, *Bullet Train* features Bad Bunny in a small but memorable role as a Mexican assassin known as "The Wolf."

Bad Bunny wasn't on-screen for very long in *Bullet Train*, but he certainly made an impression. In fact, many Bad Bunny fans took to social media after seeing the film, upset that he didn't have a bigger role in it!

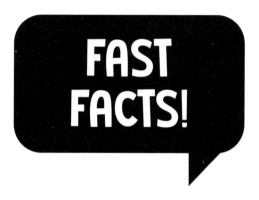

FAST FACTS!

In *Bullet Train*, Bad Bunny was credited under his real name, Benito Antonio Martínez Ocasio.

Bad Bunny had three weeks of training and fight choreography to get ready for the action sequences in *Bullet Train*.

He Really Puts on a Show!

In May 2022, Bad Bunny released his fourth solo studio album, *Un Verano Sin Ti*. As he told the hosts of the talk show *The View*, the songs on the album were created to remind him of his summers growing up as a child. The theme of "summer" would be very important to *Un Verano Sin Ti*. In fact, in English, the album's title translates to "A Summer Without You."

And in the summer of 2022, Bad Bunny went on tour to promote the album. This series of live performances was called the "World's Hottest Tour."

Bad Bunny always puts on a great live show. During some of the tour dates in the "World's Hottest Tour," he decided to have no guest stars and no featured artists. He just sang and rapped directly to the audience, and it was an intimate, special experience for the folks who attended.

On the other hand, in previous tours, Bad Bunny's live performances sometimes involved fireworks and guest stars like Jhayco and J Balvin.

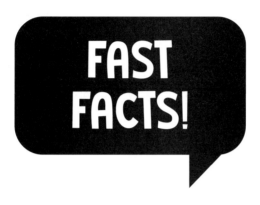

FAST FACTS!

In March 2023, *Un Verano Sin Ti* won the Grammy Award for Best Música Urbana Album.

For many of the tour dates on the "World's Hottest Tour," Bad Bunny brought out up-and-coming Puerto Rican musicians onstage as guest artists, such as trans singer and rapper Villano Antillano.

Did You Know That . . .

1 In 2021, Bad Bunny appeared backstage at WWE Monday Night Raw.

2 Bad Bunny also name-checked wrestler Eddie Guerrero on his collaboration with Cardi B, "I Like It."

3 And Bad Bunny got wrestler Booker T to appear in the music video for the *Último Tour del Mundo* song named after him.

4 In 2023, some wrestling fans took to social media to call for a match between rapper-wrestler Bad Bunny and influencer-wrestler Logan Paul.

5 But at the time of this writing, no such match has been set up.

6 *Bullet Train* director David Leitch thought that Bad Bunny did a good job in the film because of his dance background and his understanding of choreography.

7 This extended to the *fight* choreography Bad Bunny had to learn for the film.

8 David Leitch has also said that the character of the Wolf was originally going to be played by an old man. But when he saw that Bad Bunny was interested in playing the role, he changed the script, making the character a young man.

9 *Bullet Train* is based on the 2010 novel *Maria Beetle* by author Kōtarō Isaka.

10 In *Bullet Train*, Brad Pitt's character is named Ladybug.

What Makes You Laugh?

"Since childhood, I've been a clown. I've always liked being very funny or trying to make people laugh. It's my original self."

—Bad Bunny on being funny

Who or what makes you laugh? Write about it on the lines below.

_____

_____

_____

_____

_____

_____

_____

_____

_____

_____

_____

_____

_____

_____

_____

_____

_____

_____

_____

Action Star

    Bad Bunny has acted in movies and television shows. He's even been in a couple of action movies. If you were to act in a movie, what kind of movie would it be? A comedy? A historical drama? A science fiction film? A superhero movie? Something else entirely? Write about it on the lines below.

_____

_____

_____

_____

_____

_____

_____

_____

_____

_____

_____

_____

_____

_____

_____

_____

_____

Quick Quiz: Exploring New Areas

1) **Which WWE Hall of Famer called Bad Bunny the "greatest celebrity wrestler of all time"?**

   a. Sid the Science Kid
   b. Bill Nye the Science Guy
   c. Science Officer Spock
   d. Mark Henry

2) **In his cameo in the film *F9: The Fast Saga*, Bad Bunny plays the role of a ____.**

   a. Rabbit
   b. Bunny
   c. Lookout
   d. Hare

3) **The music video for Bad Bunny's song "Where She Goes" includes a brief appearance by the soccer player ____.**

   a. Ronaldinho
   b. Cobra Commander
   c. Destro
   d. Serpentor

4) In February 2021, Bad Bunny appeared as a musical guest on which iconic television show?

a. Fun with Coleslaw
b. Saturday Night Live
c. Fun with Mustard
d. Fun with Ketchup

5) In November of 2022, Bad Bunny was named Artist of the Year by ____ ____.

a. The Autobots
b. The Decepticons
c. The Dinobots
d. Apple Music

Check your answers on page 78!

Part V

ON WITH THE SHOW
Good Bunny

Bad Bunny may be largely known for his contributions to the music industry, but he's also contributed to many charitable organizations and causes over the years. And he's certainly never forgotten where he came from or who he is. In 2018, Bad Bunny gave $100,000 to the SER Telethon in Puerto Rico, to benefit children with disabilities.

More recently, he has also started a nonprofit charitable organization called the Good Bunny Foundation. In December of 2022, through this organization, Bad Bunny held a Bonita Tradición (in English, "Beautiful Tradition") gift drive in San Juan, Puerto Rico, to help those who are less fortunate. He gave out twenty thousand gifts (paint materials, musical instruments, sports equipment, and more) to the kids who attended the drive.

In 2017, shortly after Hurricanes Irma and Maria hit Puerto Rico, Bad Bunny personally distributed generators, food, and water to his hometown.

At the Bonita Tradición gift drive, dancers, drummers, and stilt walkers greeted guests as they arrived at the event.

An Ever-Evolving Artist

Like many musicians, Bad Bunny is always evolving, as an artist and as a person. Although he wasn't known for his fashion sense at the beginning of his career, these days, he's a style icon. In fact, in May 2023, Bad Bunny was considered one of the best dressed celebrities at the Met Gala.

Over the years, he has also become increasingly outspoken about social and political issues involving Puerto Rico.

For instance, in September 2022, Bad Bunny put an unusual video on his YouTube channel. The video began with a music video for his song "El Apagón" (in English, "The Blackout"). But after about three minutes, it transitioned to *Aquí Vive Gente* ("People Live Here"), an eighteen-minute documentary by a journalist named Bianca Graulau. *Aquí Vive Gente* is about injustices in the Puerto Rican real estate industry. As explained in the video, some low-income residents of San Juan were being evicted in order to make room for wealthy people and their expensive houses. In sharing this video, Bad Bunny used his platform to spread awareness about this unfair and terrible situation.

What will Bad Bunny do next? That remains to be seen. After all, part of Bad Bunny's appeal is that he's unpredictable.

But whatever his next project is, it's sure to get everyone talking!

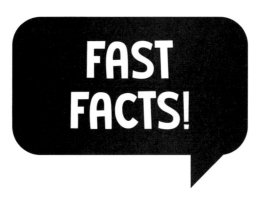

FAST FACTS!

For a time, Bad Bunny was attached to star as the title character in *El Muerto*, a Marvel movie about a wrestler-supervillain.

However, in June 2023, Sony, the movie studio behind the film, removed the movie from their schedule. Now the project's status is unknown.

Did You Know That . . .

1 The 2022 Bonita Tradición gift drive was held at the Coliseo Roberto Clemente in San Juan.

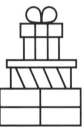

2 The event also included live music, food stations, face painting, a pig roast, and a chance to get a photo op with Bad Bunny!

3 Bad Bunny's album *Un Verano Sin Ti* ended 2022 as the most streamed album on Spotify *globally*.

4 It was also the most streamed album *in the US* for that year, making it more frequently streamed than offerings from Harry Styles and Olivia Rodrigo.

5 On December 22, 2022, Bad Bunny released his new track, "Gato de Noche" (in English, "Cat at Night").

6 "Gato de Noche" was a collaboration with fellow recording artist Ñengo Flow.

7 Bad Bunny was named *Billboard*'s Top Artist of 2022.

8 It was the first time an artist who primarily records their music in Spanish became the year's top artist.

9 In the fall of 2020, during the pandemic, Bad Bunny drove through New York City neighborhoods, performing for his fans while standing on a trailer made up to look like a subway car.

10 When he did this, fans chased after the trailer, eager to get close to Bad Bunny.

The Story of Your Life

"[I]t's funny and also frustrating to see how people really think they know about the lives of celebrities, of what they think, of what they do day to day. They think they know the story of your life, your interior thoughts, your romantic life, but, in reality, they don't know at all…"

—Bad Bunny on the story of his life

If you were to summarize the story of your life in just a few sentences, how would you do it? Write about it on the lines below.

_____
_____
_____
_____
_____
_____
_____
_____
_____
_____
_____
_____
_____
_____
_____
_____
_____
_____
_____
_____
_____
_____

Charitable Causes

Bad Bunny has given money to various charities. That's why he set up the Good Bunny Foundation. Is there a charity you're particularly passionate about? Write about it on the lines below.

_____

_____

_____

_____

_____

_____

_____

_____

_____

_____

_____

_____

_____

_____

_____

_____

_____

ANSWER KEY

Pages 18–19:
1) d, 2) a, 3) c, 4) b, 5) d

Pages 34–35:
1) c, 2) a, 3) d, 4) b, 5) c

Pages 50–51:
1) a, 2) d, 3) b, 4) c, 5) c

Pages 66–67:
1) d, 2) c, 3) a, 4) b, 5) d

Arie Kaplan began his career writing about pop music for magazines such as *Teen Beat*, *Tiger Beat*, and *BOP*. And over the years, he has satirized pop music as a writer for *MAD Magazine*. Arie is also the author of the juvenile nonfiction book *American Pop: Hit Makers, Superstars, and Dance Revolutionaries*.

As a nonfiction author, Arie is perhaps most well-known for the acclaimed book *From Krakow to Krypton: Jews and Comic Books*, a 2008 finalist for the National Jewish Book Award. He has also penned numerous books and graphic novels for young readers, including *LEGO Star Wars: The Official Stormtrooper Training Manual*, *The New Kid from Planet Glorf*, *Jurassic Park Little Golden Book*, *Frankie and the Dragon*, and *Swashbuckling Scoundrels: Pirates in Fact and Fiction*. Aside from his work as an author, Arie is a screenwriter for television, video games, and transmedia. Please check out his website: www.ariekaplan.com.